MAKING MUSIC

I0895124

Written by Bernadette Parkhurst-Smith

THE SCIENCE OF WOODWIND INSTRUMENTS

KidHaven PUBLISHING

Published in 2027 by
KidHaven Publishing, an Imprint of Greenhaven Publishing, LLC
2544 Clinton St., Buffalo, NY 14224

© 2026 BookLife Publishing Ltd.

Written by: Bernadette Parkhurst-Smith
Edited by: Rebecca Phillips-Bartlett
Designed by: Ker Ker Lee

All facts, statistics, web addresses, and URLs in this book were verified as valid and accurate at time of writing. No responsibility for any changes to external websites or references can be accepted by either the author or publisher.

Cataloging-in-Publication Data

Names: Parkhurst-Smith, Bernadette.
Title: The science of woodwind instruments / Bernadette Parkhurst-Smith.
Description: Buffalo, NY : KidHaven Publishing, 2027. | Series: Making music | Includes glossary and index.
Identifiers: ISBN 9781534570252 (pbk.) | ISBN 9781534570269 (library bound) | ISBN 9781534570276 (ebook)
Subjects: LCSH: Woodwind instruments--Juvenile literature.
Classification: LCC ML931.P375 2027 | DDC 788.219--dc23

All rights reserved.
No part of this book may be reproduced in any form without permission in writing from the publisher, except by a reviewer.

Printed in China

CPSIA compliance information: Batch #QS27KH: For further information contact Greenhaven Publishing LLC at 1-844-317-7404.

Please visit our website, www.greenhavenpublishing.com.
For a free color catalog of all our high-quality books, call toll free 1-844-317-7404 or fax 1-844-317-7405.

Find us on

Photo Credits – Images courtesy of Shutterstock.com, unless otherwise stated.

Cover & Recurring – RidiUmbrella, hatsak, Mariia Korneeva. 2–3 – Yuriy Golub. 4–5 – ViDI Studio, Jack.Q. 6–7 – SvetaZi, Ezume Images. 8–9 – Pavel Sazonov, Harold Diaz Lara. 10–11 – metamorworks, sirtravelalot. 12–13 – Krysja, Euroscript AB. 14–15 – wavebreakmedia, Mikhail Olykainen. 16–17 – NOVODIASTOCK, Toritseju Ogbebor. 18–19 – Gulf MG, Fabio Pagani. 20–21 – VeronArt16, Zhuravlev Andrey. 22–23 – WR7, Kruglov_Orda, Jalisko, Venn-Photo, Stock Up.

CONTENTS

Words that look like this can be found in the glossary on page 24.

SCIENCE AND SOUNDS

Music is full of wonderful sounds that make us feel happy, sad, or excited. But how do instruments make these sounds? There is no mystery here. The answer can be explained with science!

Let's learn about what happens when we play musical instruments!

This book is all about woodwind instruments. These are wind instruments, which means you blow air into them to make a sound. Many woodwind instruments are actually made of metal, plastic, or ceramics, not wood.

Woodwind instruments all look very different from each other.

WHAT IS SOUND?

Sounds are vibrations. Vibrations are small, quick movements that go back and forth. Vibrations travel through the air, like waves travel through water. When our ears pick up these vibrations, they hear the sound.

As sound moves through the air, it is called a sound wave.

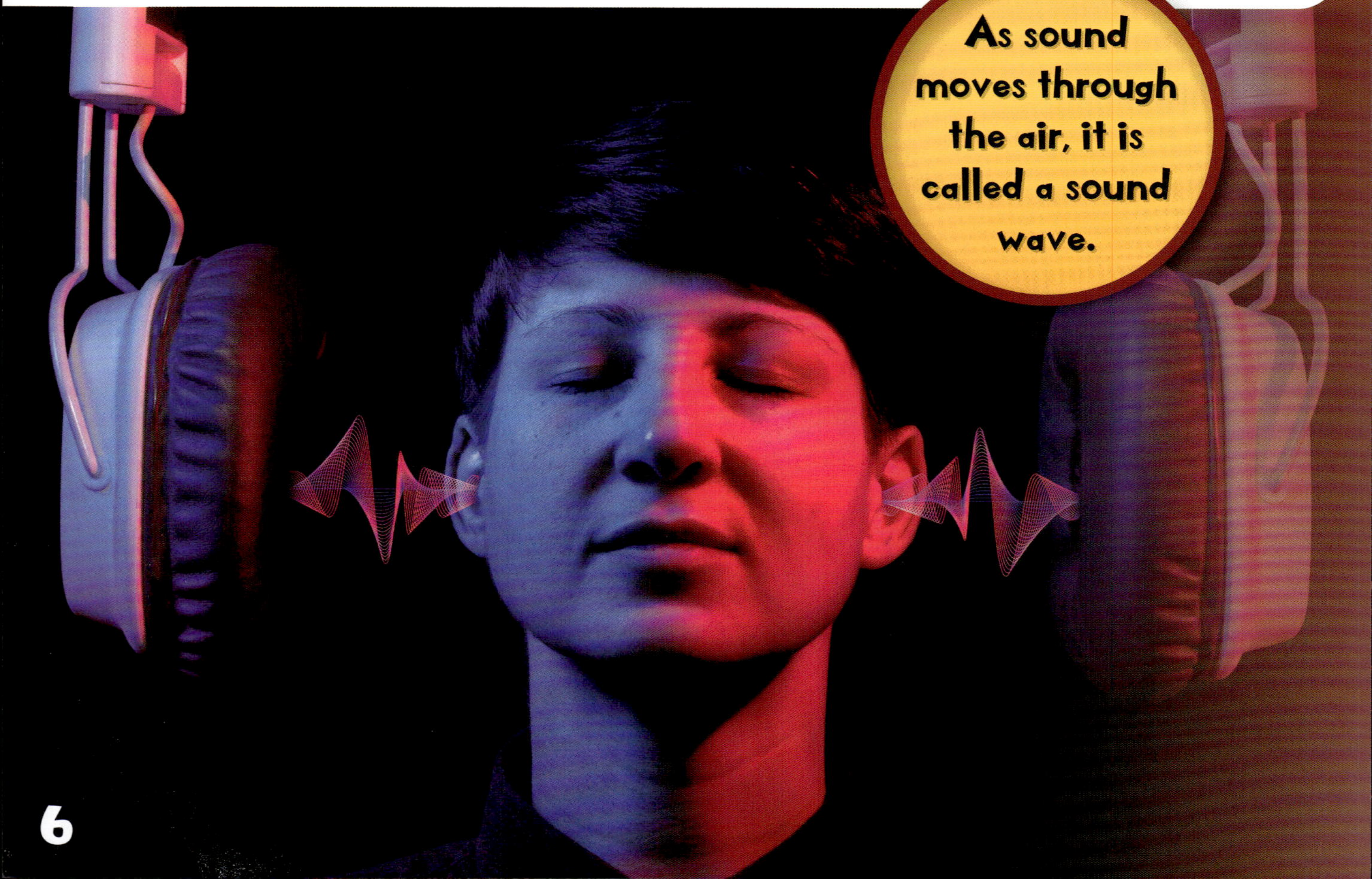

Woodwind instruments are hollow tubes, meaning there is air inside. When you blow into them, vibrations are made. These vibrations create a sound wave. The musical sound that you hear is called a note.

Let's see how different woodwind instruments make the air vibrate.

CLARINET

A clarinet has a reed in the mouthpiece. Blowing into the mouthpiece makes the reed vibrate, which then vibrates the air inside too. Reeds are usually made from a type of plant called cane.

The end of the clarinet is called the bell. The bell's shape helps the sound waves coming out of the instrument get to your ears. It makes the clarinet sound louder.

SAXOPHONE

A saxophone also has a reed. Like other woodwinds, it has holes along its body too. Air can escape through these holes. You change the pitch of the note by pressing keys, which cover the holes.

Saxophones are often made of a metal alloy called brass.

Covering holes means the sound wave travels farther down the saxophone. The more holes you cover, the more air the sound wave travels through. This makes the pitch lower. Open holes make a higher pitch.

Saxophones are famous for playing a style of music called jazz.

BASSOON

A bassoon is a double reed instrument. To play it, you blow into two reeds tied together. It also has lots of holes that are covered or uncovered to change the pitch.

Bassoons are the biggest woodwind instruments in an orchestra.

Bassoons are big. The body is long and bends around. The bell, where the sound comes out, is on top. Big instruments, like bassoons, have lots of air inside, which means they can play low notes.

FLUTE

A flute is a small, thin instrument. It can play very high notes. To make a sound, you blow across a hole at the top, and the air hits the edge of the hole.

Flutes are usually made of metal or wood.

Some of the air you blow goes into the flute. Some of the air goes over the top. This splitting of air creates a vibration. This vibration becomes the sound that comes out of the instrument.

Some of the first flutes were made of bone around 35,000 years ago.

RECORDER

Recorders come in lots of different sizes. When you blow into a recorder, the flow of air hits a sharp edge. The sharp edge splits the air, which creates vibrations.

Smaller recorders make higher notes. Bigger recorders make lower notes.

You can change the loudness of a sound by how hard or soft you blow. When you blow hard, you create bigger vibrations, which make a louder sound. Blowing softly creates smaller vibrations and quieter sounds.

Recorders are usually made of wood or plastic.

BAGPIPES

Bagpipes have around five pipes. Three of these pipes are usually drones. Each drone normally has a single reed. Another pipe is the chanter. The chanter has a reed and holes to change pitch.

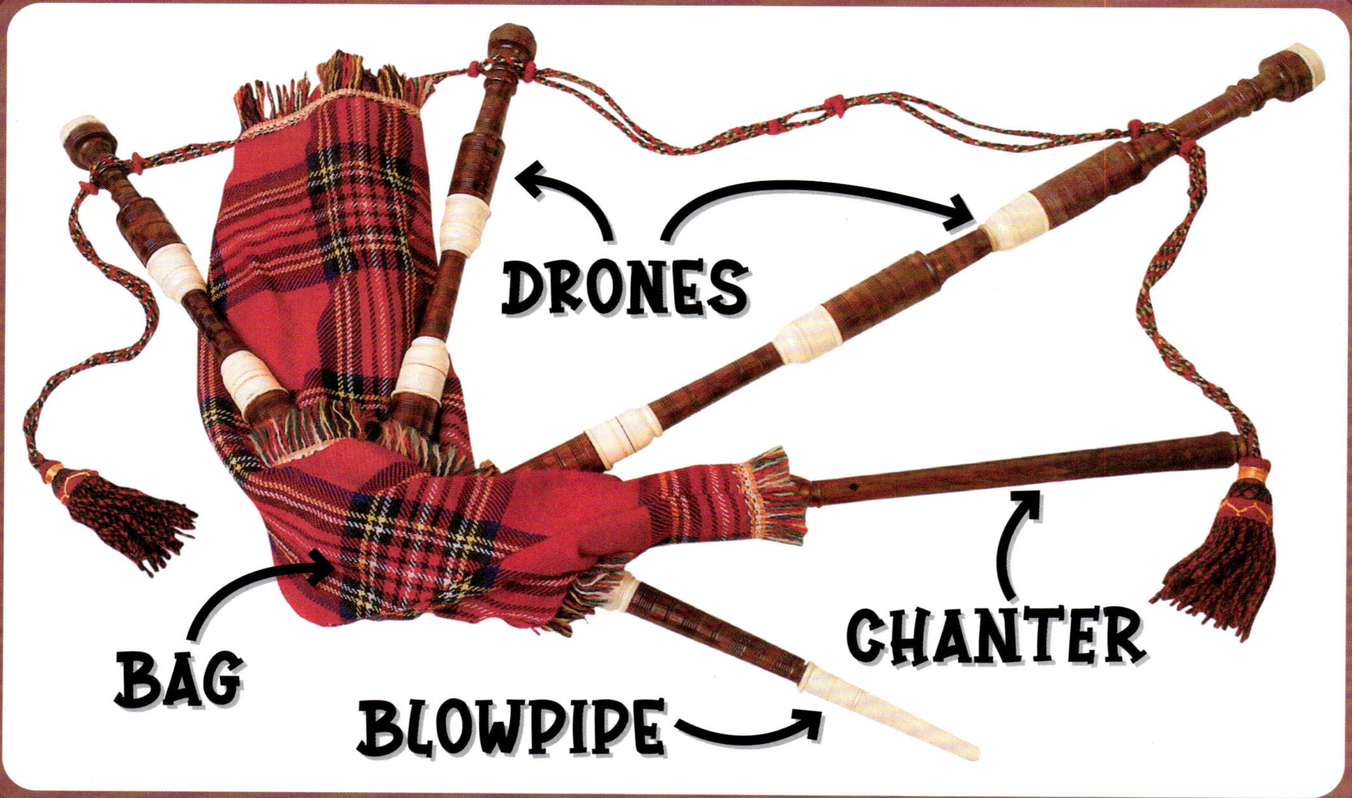

You blow into the blowpipe to get air into the bag. By pressing on the bag with your arm, air is squeezed into all the pipes together, so you can play many notes at once.

The chanter pipe plays the melody because it can play different notes.

OCARINA

An ocarina is a small woodwind instrument. It is a different shape than most instruments. Instead of being a tube, it is more rounded. It has finger holes to change the pitch and a sharp edge inside.

Ocarinas come in many different sizes.

Ocarinas are mostly ceramic. Sometimes they are made of metal or plastic. Ocarinas were first made thousands of years ago in Central America. Some ocarinas from the past were made to sound like birds.

HARMONICA

A harmonica is a very small instrument. It has lots of little holes, and each one makes a different note. You play it by blowing or sucking air, which vibrates metal reeds inside.

Changing your mouth shape can change the pitch. This is known as bending the note.

Now you know how woodwinds create sound. What sounds would you like to make? Pick an instrument and start practicing. Soon you will be making music!

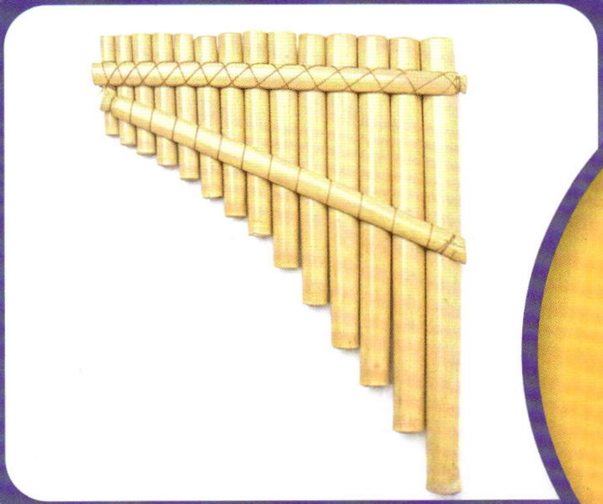

Pan flutes are woodwind instruments. Could you make your own pan flute with everyday items?

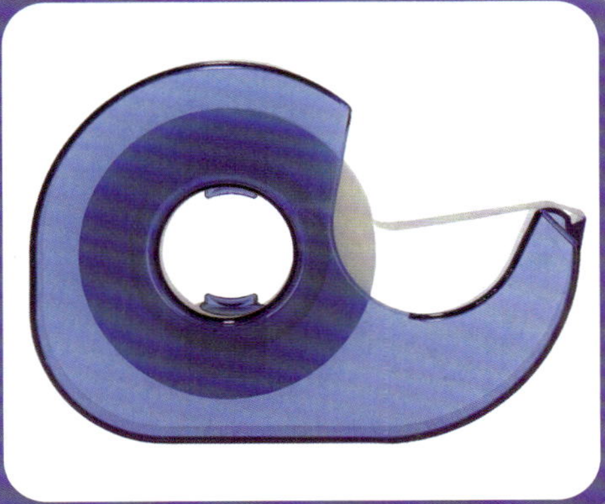

ARY

something made from mixing two or more metals

ica a place in the lower part of North America

s clay that has been heated

ollow not full, has air or empty space inside

keys in woodwind instruments, keys are small levers and pads, often made of metal, that help cover holes

melody the main tune of the music, which is often the part you remember and sing along to

mouthpiece in music, it is the part of the instrument you blow air into

orchestra a group of musicians who play a certain style of music called classical, which usually involves a particular list of instruments

pitch how high or low a musical note is: high notes can be squeaky, while low notes are deeper

INDEX